THE CHECKERED HISTORY *of the* CIRCUMSCRIPTION THEORY

Robert L. Carneiro

authorHOUSE®

AuthorHouse™
1663 Liberty Drive
Bloomington, IN 47403
www.authorhouse.com
Phone: 1 (800) 839-8640

Published by AuthorHouse 05/10/2018

ISBN: 978-1-5462-3994-9 (sc)
ISBN: 978-1-5462-3995-6 (e)

Print information available on the last page.

THE CHECKERED HISTORY OF THE CIRCUMSCRIPTION THEORY

by Robert L. Carneiro

Were you to ask an anthropologist what one word he would most readily associate with my name, the word he would most likely choose would be "circumscription." That is the word which most distinctly refers to a theory of the origin of the state I proposed nearly half a century ago.

In the intervening years the theory has gained a certain currency in anthropology and may even be considered the leading theory among those purporting to account for the rise of the state.

The emergence of the state out of simpler forms of political organization did not occur easily since it took the human race some two million years to bring it about. But once attained, the state opened the gates to a prodigious elaboration of culture that would have been impossible otherwise.

I do not intend to discuss my theory in exhaustive detail here beyond saying what is needed to make its essential features known to those unfamiliar with it. Rather, I propose to narrate the story of how the theory came to be and to tell something of its convoluted history.

First, though, it is necessary to present something of the background against which the theory and its development can best be understood.

In the latter half of the 19th century the classical evolutionists, principally Herbert Spencer and Lewis H. Morgan, were much concerned with political organization and how higher forms of it had grown out of simpler ones. In the fateful year of 1896, however, Franz Boas fired the opening salvo of what proved to be several decades of sustained and unrelenting anti-evolution. During that period anthropologists essentially turned their backs on evolutionary questions such as how the state had arisen, preferring instead to direct their efforts toward matters of lesser magnitude.

True, in 1927 Robert H. Lowie published *The Origin of the State,* but despite its title the book did not propose anything like a coherent theory of how the state had arisen. Rather, much of the book was devoted to poking holes in attempts by others to do so.

Consequently one can say that by the middle of the twentieth century hardly a theory could be seen on the anthropological landscape that offered a step-by-step account of how, beginning as simple autonomous villages, human societies had gradually formed larger and more complex political units, culminating in the rise off the state.

In those days, clouded over by an anti-evolutionary miasma, if anything could be said to pass for a theory of the origin of the state it was what I have called the "automatic theory." As best we can extract it from the writings of archaeologists like Robert Braidwood and V. Gordon Childe, it ran somewhat as follows.

The invention of agriculture made it possible for food surpluses to be produced, permitting certain individuals to be withdrawn from primary food production and devote themselves to non-subsistence activities. In doing so they became specialists in all manner of arts and crafts, as well as in other sorts of activities such as those that developed into the political and religious institutions characterizing the early state.

Essentially that was all there was to it. There seemed to be little awareness that in accounting for the rise of the state from a level of simple villages the central problem was how community autonomy, which had characterized human society for the previous two million years, was to be transcended and replaced by multi-community polities. Once this critical step had been taken, though, a series of developments followed which saw successively larger political units being formed until one of sufficient size and complexity had emerged to which the term "state" could be applied.

But the automatic theory failed to see that it was the mechanism—the instrumentality—that enabled this advance to occur that had to be identified and its operation described before the state could be said to have emerged.

And this development entailed more than the ability to produce a surplus of food.

There was one notable exception to the bland acceptance of the automatic theory. In the pages of *Oriental Despotism* Karl Wittfogel advanced the *hydraulic hypothesis*, the main idea of which was this: In certain arid regions of the world, where irrigation was necessary to make agriculture possible, the political machinery required to operate such an irrigation system was, of necessity, an instrument of social control. And, growing in scale and power, this instrument eventually became the state.

This theory had some standing until it was shown that a state organization had first to be in place before an irrigation system of substantial size could be made to work.

There was, I should note, a bit of truth in Wittfogel's theory. Or rather, there was a false correlation which disguised an underlying truth. What Wittfogel attributed to aridity can more fundamentally be attributed—as we shall soon see—to *environmental circumscription*.

Thus before the year 1970, let us say, it could be said that no robust, fine-grained theory of primary state formation was to be found in anthropology.

During the 1940s and 1950s Leslie White had effectively pruned away much of the anti-evolutionary undergrowth that for so long had hindered theoretical advances in anthropology, especially as had pertained to cultural evolution.

But while he was a dragon-slayer of the anti-evolutionary chimera, White was not concerned to the same degree with erecting in the barren terrain left over any solid and substantial structures to replace what had been demolished. There was no clear description in his essays, brilliant as they were, of the way societies had advanced, step by step and stage by stage, along the pathway from initial simplicity to the extraordinary complexity of the modern age.

White, however, did deal incisively with what had powered this advance, arguing that, above all, it was the harnessing of energy that had brought this advance about. Again, though, he did not set forth in any detail the successive phases of this progression.

Thus when I came to be interested in the problem of primary state formation I found that, to a large extent, the field still lay fallow, waiting to be sown.

As a graduate student in anthropology at the University of Michigan under Leslie White, I had acquired an evolutionary perspective and been infused with a corresponding zeal to pursue it. That did not mean, of course, that from the start I was eager to formulate a theory of how the first state had arisen. However, having majored in political science as an undergraduate I was aware, if only vaguely, that the origin of the state was a problem of long standing. Moreover, from my study of anthropology—in whose domain this problem most fully lay—I knew that no adequate solution to it had yet emerged.

It was certainly not the case, however, that when the time came to engage in field work this problem was uppermost in my mind. My intention was simply to carry out a conventional piece of field research covering most aspects of Kuikuru culture, emphasizing whatever part of it I found particularly interesting.

This turned out to be slash-and-burn cultivation focusing on the growing of manioc, the Kuikuru's staple crop. Manioc cultivation, as practiced by them was notable for its large and reliable yields which allowed the men considerable time left over after subsistence, during which they could engage in a variety of non-subsistence activities.

The impressive nature of Kuikuru manioc yields stayed with me after I left the field. And when I began reading about subsistence practices among other South American societies, especially the Inca (whose staple crop was maize) I was struck by the fact that when the two systems of agriculture were compared, that of the Kuikuru— based on manioc cultivation—showed itself to be substantially more productive. And this advantage was present whether we measured productivity per unit of land or per unit of labor.

This I found highly relevant, in a negative way, when trying to explain why the Inca had achieved a society so much more advanced than that of the Kuikuru even though their agriculture was distinctly less productive. And this fact continued to intrigue me. It forced me to conclude that any facile explanation purporting to explain the rise of the Inca state based largely on economic factors had to be reexamined, and eventually to be discarded.

With regard to the matter of finding a satisfactory explanation of how the state arisen, therefor, there remained a theoretical vacuum. This vacuum needed to be filled, but with what?

The solution I hit upon came to me while I was teaching at the University of Wisconsin in the spring of 1957. I clearly recall that my first mention of it to anyone was to my colleague C. W. M. Hart at lunch one day. And his response remains engraved on my mind.

Having explained my theory to him I

said that after looking at examples of early state formation beyond South America it appeared that the theory held up in other parts of the world as well.

Hart had never been a student of Franz Boas but his reaction was very much in the Boasian mold. No sooner had I remarked on the theory's nearly univers**a**l application than he exclaimed—almost hopefully, it seemed—"We don't know enough about the central Congo, and if we did, we might find an exception "to it there."

For Hart, it appeared, the exception was more noble than the rule!

*   *   *

But having avoided stating the theory outright up to this point, let me now turn to it directly. The solution to the problem of state formation did not occur to me suddenly. There was no epiphany, no

Eureka moment. However, when it finally took shape in my mind, in the spring of 1957, I regarded it as compelling enough to warrant writing down a brief summary of it and dating it.

I wasn't particularly concerned with establishing my priority in the matter because in those days hardly anyone was seriously trying to account for the origin of the state.

Since economic factors appeared not to hold the key to why large and complex polities had arisen in the Andes but not in the Amazon, I started looking at other factors and soon focused on warfare.

Warfare was endemic to both Amazonia and the Andes, but when closely examined it could be seen to differ significantly in the two areas, both in its causes and its scale, but particularly in its consequences.

In Amazonia, large, unbroken tracts of

rainforest extended from the Atlantic to the the Andes, so that virtually no part of it was unsuited to manioc cultivation. In war therefor a defeated village could avoid subjugation by its stronger enemies by simply moving away and establishing itself in a new location, continuing to live much as before. By virtue of its mobility an Amazonian village was thus able to remain independent and autonomous.

This process of "fight and flight" acted to preserve throughout Amazonia a regimen of village autonomy. Only in a few areas with unusual ecological conditions were chiefdoms—multi-village polities—able to arise. Thus no further political development was to be expected.

In the Andean region, however, things were markedly different. There, conditions favoring political evolution were present, most conspicuously so on the coast of Peru.

The many narrow valleys produced by rivers knifing their way down the western slopes of the Andes were flanked by the driest desert in the world. The arable land enclosed within each valley was therefore not only restricted in size but sharply bounded along its perimeter.

The natural increase in human numbers that occurred over time, gave rise in these pockets of land to population pressure. This could not be relieved as it could have been by simply having a defeated village move away, as in Amazonia. This pressure caused an increase in the frequency of warfare.

But with the desert providing no refuge, defeated groups were forced to stay in place and be subjugated by their stronger neighbors. At first this subjugation might entail little more than the payment of an annual tribute, but eventually it resulted in complete loss of sovereignty. And with that came the emergence of the first multi-village polities in the region—chiefdoms.

Autonomous villages were thus diminished in number, being largely replaced by the chiefdoms that had defeated and absorbed them.

Warfare, which was now mostly between the chiefdoms that had now emerged, was often waged for outright conquest. And as one chiefdom defeated and incorporated another, the result was the formation of larger and larger chiefdoms. And as the stronger ones defeated the weaker ones, here and there valley-wide kingdoms began to emerge along the coast. Several of them became kingdoms ruled by men whose power and wealth are attested to by the opulence of the grave goods that accompanied them in their tombs.

The polities over which these men ruled had attained a size and complexity that warranted their being recognized as full fledged states.

Warfare, which continued and intensified, was now often waged between such kingdoms, the result being the formation of even larger polities. It wasn't long before several multi-valley kingdoms had emerged on the coast of Peru.

Continuing to be fought, war now involved increasingly larger polities, including those of the highlands. A century or so before the arrival of the Spaniards these wars culminated in the formation of a single huge state—the Inca empire.

*   *   *

But, having carried political evolution to the point of early state formation, our purpose has been achieved. There is no need here to carry our account of political evolution any further.

What I have attempted to portray can be summarized as follows. Warfare, which continued in areas of circumscribed arable land, led, step by step, to the supersedence of autonomous villages and the establishment of states.

In Amazonia, in contrast with the Andes, environmental circumscription was essentially lacking. Thus political evolution rarely reached the level of chiefdoms and never went beyond that.

In other regions of the world where the state had emerged, the circumscription theory seemed to hold up well: the valleys of Mexico and Oaxaca in Mesoamerica, the Nile and Tigris-Euphrates valleys in the Near East, the Indus valley; and the upper Yellow River valley in China, where the Chinese state first arose, were all regions where agriculture was practiced but where the arable land was sharply limited by environmental features.

So here was a theory that appeared to explain primary state formation, in various regions of the world, better than the reigning theories of the day, such as they were.

But I continued to pursue the problem of state formation. The year following the crystallization of the circumscription theory in my mind I happened to read Jacques Barrau's study of subsistence agriculture in Melanesia which seemed to solidify the theory further. Barrau showed that slash-and-burn agriculture was not necessarily a dead end, as was generally regarded. Under population pressure, shifting cultivation was intensified and was able to produce the higher yields needed to feed the increasing numbers of people. Yet areas of Melanesia where such higher yields had been attained had not developed states or anything close to it. So again, here was evidence that it took more than heightened agricultural production to allow the state to come into existence.

Up to this point not a word of the circumscription theory had appeared in print. Then in 1959 the opportunity presented itself to take the first steps in that direction. This occurred during a symposium on subsistence agriculture in South America presented at the annual meeting of the American Anthropological Association held that year in Mexico City. While most of my paper in that symposium was meant to counter the views of Betty Meggers regarding the supposed limitations imposed by a rainforest environment on cultural development, I used the rest of the paper to introduce the circumscription theory.

It was not, however, the formal, expanded

presentation of it I had envisioned writing at some point, but at least it laid out the essential elements of the theory.

It was in this paper that I introduced the word "circumscription," which has come to label the theory as a whole.

This paper, along with several others in the symposium, was published a year later in a special publication of the Venezuelan journal *Antropologica*.

Still, nothing was spurring me on to write a full account of the theory. What finally did so was reading a discussion of my theory by Malcolm Webb, an archaeologist at the University of New Orleans, who looked at the great sweep of prehistory in evolutionary terms, as I did. Webb had evidently read my article in *Antropologica*. Moreover, since I knew him personally I may have discussed the theory with him at some point. At any rate, his treatment of the theory was both informed and sympathetic but somehow it seemed inappropriate for me to allow someone else to give the theory its first general airing instead of doing so myself.

Again, though, I failed to put pen to paper.

The impetus to actually begin working on the article I had so long envisioned came shortly thereafter during a lunch with Elizabeth Knappman, who had just begun working as an editor for Natural History Press. This publishing venture had recently been formed as a consortium between the Museum and Doubleday. Like a true acquisitions editor, Knappman was on the prowl for manuscripts. But the only thing I had to offer at the time was the circumscription theory, and we both agreed that, whatever its merits, the theory did not warrant having an entire book devoted to it. However Knappman thought it would make an interesting article for *Natural History* magazine, in those days published by the Museum. Accordingly I got in touch with Alfred Meyer and his assistant editor and we agreed to discuss the matter. We met for lunch at a restaurant near Lincoln Center, and after studying the menu I ordered steak tartar. Now, I like my meat very well done, so when a large plate of raw beef was set in front of me, I blanched. But not wanting to admit my ignorance or to show the white feather, I forced myself to gulp down the whole thing. Little did I suspect that this small misadventure would prove to be an omen of things to come!

I described the circumscription theory to Meyer and his assistant editor and we discussed the possibility of my writing an article about it. Meyer said it might make an interesting piece for the magazine. We parted with my having a clear understanding that I was to prepare a draft of the article as my up the theory as my time permitted and, when finished, submit it.

I was pleased with the outcome of the meeting and the prospect that the circumscription theory would soon see the light of print. Still, I was in no hurry to start working on the manuscript since I had other fish to fry.

As I recall, our luncheon took place in late November. Then, about a month later, I got a frantic phone call from Mayer asking where my article was, saying that he had scheduled it for the February issue of the magazine, that space had already been allotted to it, and that nothing could be put in its place.

'Od's bodikins!

I didn't even have a draft of the paper ready. That wasn't my understanding. I thought I was to write the article at my leisure and submit it only when it was ready. But if the article was indeed scheduled for the February issue and there was nothing to run in its place, then, like a good soldier I would have something ready for Al by the date he really needed it.

So for the next three weeks I put everything else aside and worked on the article as intensely as I could. I finished the thing and submitted it to *Natural History,* looking forward to seeing the circumscription theory, at long last, make itself known to the world.

And then I waited.

One day, two days, three days. Nothing. Not a word from Al Meyer. Was he pleased with it? Did he propose any changes in it?

At last I called the assistant editor and asked about the status of things. He hemmed and hawed and I knew right away something was amiss. Finally he came out with it. Al had decided not to run my article after all. Despite what he had told me, he had found something else to run in its place.

I gnashed my teeth but held my tongue.

Talking with curators who had also worked with **Natural History** I soon learned that my experience was by no means unique. Others had suffered a similar fate at the hands of Al Meyer… It was his *modus operandi.* Hold out the bright prospect of publication and then take it away.

But it was not a total loss. At least I now had a manuscript in hand. The vessel, with a goodly cargo on board, had finally slipped anchor and set sail. Only now its port of destination was uncertain.

The question then was, with *Natural History* out of the picture, where should I now direct the manuscript?

It didn't take much thought to decide. The journal that came immediately to mind was *Science,* which in those days often published articles dealing with the development of the early civilizations, both in the Old World and the New. And since my article could be said to lay down the foundations on which those civilizations were built, it seemed an appropriate place for it.

As the flagship journal of the American Association for the Advancement of Science, it was a publication with a wide readership in the scientific community, including anthropology, and enjoyed high prestige. Thus to have my article appear in its pages would be highly desirable. Indeed it would be the perfect place for it. But would *Science* accept it?

Now an article written for *Natural History* magazine would not do for *Science.* Clearly the article had to be rewritten. More solid flesh had to be put on the bare bones of the theory. The argument had to be more sharply chiseled. Additional data had to be incorporated, and references—out of place in *Natural History*—supplied. In short the article had to bear, conspicuously but not obtrusively, the usual hallmarks of scholarship, characteristics not particularly evident in its first incarnation.

In the process of revising the paper I introduced into it two new elements: *resource concentration* and *social circumscription*.

In the years that had passed since the theory had first taken shape it had become clear to me that in certain parts of the world, such as the area of the Olmec in southern Mexico, the rich concentration of wild food resources, mainly fish, had drawn people to it in large numbers, creating population pressure not unlike that occurring under environmental circumscription in agricultural areas when the arable land had run out. Thus it seemed important to add resource concentration to the theory.

The second element added—social circumscription—was suggested to me by Napoleon Chagnon based on his field experience with the Yanomamo in Venezuela. He had observed that the Shamatari, a subgroup of Yanomamo, had larger villages that were located closer together than was the case in other Yanomamo regions. Furthermore the Shamatari were also more warlike and had stronger political leadership than did other Yanomamo groups. The closer spacing of Shamatari villages seemed to Chagnon to have acted much as environmental circumscription in strengthening their political structure by increasing the frequency of warfare, in which the village chief took the leadership role. And Chagnon felt that "social circumscription" was an apt term for this effect.

However, while the Shamatari were moving in the direction of a more highly evolved political system, they had not proceeded very far in that direction. Moawa, a Shamatari chief, while an unusually vigorous and intimidating political leader, had not brought about even the consolidation of separate villages that mark the existence of a chiefdom.

Thus it seemed to me that the Shamatari did not constitute an especially good example of the condition which they were supposed to exemplify. Nevertheless it was reasonable to suggest, as Shamatari conditions had to Chagnon, that if actually present these conditions would certainly be conducive to the development of higher forms of political organization.

And in fact more robust examples of these conditions, coupled with a more evolved political,structure, have since come to light.

It seemed to me therefor that social circumscription was a valid and useful concept and I readily accepted it as an adjunct to the circumscription theory.

This case brings to mind an analogous one involving the principle of asymmetrical evolution. This principle was devised years ago to account for the disparities found among various parts of the skeleton of Piltdown Man. Yet even when Piltdown was shown to be a hoax, the concept of asymmetrical evolution survived the false instance that had given rise to it because genuine examples of it have since been found.

In preparing my manuscript for *Science* I took my time. There was no hurry. No one was breathing down my neck. And of course *Science* had no idea that it was coming.

When at last the manuscript was ready to submit, I sent it off under the title of "A Theory of the Origin of the State." For a time, I thought of calling it "A New Theory of the Origin of the State," but decided against it. Somehow the shorter title sounded less presumptuous. And claiming to account for a major step in social evolution was ambitious enough.

I submitted my article to *Science,* addressing it to the editor, the distinguished nuclear physicist Philip Abelson, co-discoverer of neptunium, the first trans-uranic element. The contrast between my two editors—Abelson and Meyer—could not have been greater. The difference between them was to be measured in orders of magnitude.

But again I had to wait for a reply. This

time the wait seemed even longer, and when it finally came it was—again—not what I had hoped for.

Included with Abelson's letter of rejection was the single set of reviewer's comments on the basis of which he had turned down my paper. The gist of this critic's comments was that while he thought the article was interesting and well written, it was "too speculative for *Science*."

When your article has been summarily rejected, there are two types of letter you can write to the editor.

One in which you berate him for failing to recognize the merits of your submission. The other type of letter is written when you think there is still a chance he can be made to change his mind. In the latter case you have to have to rephrase your argument more sharply while making sure to couch it in honeyed words.

My letter was of the second kind. I focused on the fact that Abelson's rejection was based on the opinion of only one reviewer as opposed to the usual two or more, and that the reviewer's main objection was that my theory was "too speculative for *Science.*"

I defended the use of speculation in science, pointing out that when one is trying to account for something that occurred thousands of years ago, with no observer present to leave an account of the process, there was no recourse but to engage in a certain amount of speculation.

I mailed my letter to Abelson and waited for his reply. Had I argued my case convincingly enough to make a difference?

But meanwhile I went off to Philadelphia to attend the annual meeting of the American Anthropological Association which was being held at the University

Museum. Like most of those in attendance, I was staying in a downtown hotel.

After one afternoon session I went out to a street corner near the Museum to wait for a bus back into town when I ran into William Sanders, a prominent archaeologist who was also going back to his hotel. We got on the same bus and began talking. I knew Bill but only slightly. Most of his work had been in Mexico but he stood out among archaeologists as one who was concerned not just with the prehistory of a particular area but also with cultural evolution on a grand scale. He had just published a major book, co-authored with Barbara Price, entitled *Mesoamerica; The Evolution of a Civilization,* which had become very influential among archaeologists.

We talked about our common interests but It was not long before I told him about the sad fate of my paper on the origin of the state which had been rejected by *Science* on the basis of only one reviewer's comments.

As I talked, Bill's eyes narrowed and finally he exclaimed, "You know, that article was sent to me for review and I liked it and urged that it be published.".

What a coincidence! And, as it turned out, what a fortunate one at that. But what could have gone wrong? Had Sanders' letter to Abelson been lost in the mail? Had it lain unopened on his desk? Either way it had played no part in Abelson's decision.

However that could now be about to change for Sanders said he would re-mail his favorable review to Abelson as soon as he got back to his office at Penn State.

I never learned how much Abelson had been swayed by my letter and how much by Sanders' favorable review. The net result though was that not many days later I received the good news from Abelson that *Science* would publish my article after all.

I was of course greatly buoyed by the news. So much so that when the time came to order reprints of my article I went overboard and ordered 300. Even before I received my supply of reprints though I knew exactly who was to receive the first one.

There's an old Spanish saying that revenge is a dish best served cold. So the first reprint I sent out bore the inscription:

"To Al Meyer, In everlasting gratitude for saving me from a terrible mistake."

My article appeared around the middle of 1970, and I have to report that the earth continued to turn serenely on its axis. But then in March of 1979 I received a letter from Robert Graber, then a graduate student at the University of Wisconsin, Milwaukee, asking me— gently—if in formulating the circumscription theory I might have been influenced by the writings of Herbert Spencer. And he enclosed some passages from Spencer's *The Principles of Sociology* which he thought might have affected my thinking on the subject before I wrote my article.

Here indeed was something to ponder

In preparing to write *The Principles of 2Sociology* Spencer had read widely in history and ethnography. And, with his quick eye for causation, he had perceived a definite relationship between particular features of the environment and the level of political organization attained there. And he voiced this relationship as follows:

"Social integration [more precisely, political consolidation] is easy [to achieve] within a territory which, while able to support a large population, affords facilities for coercing the units of that population, especially if it is bounded by regions offering little sustenance or peopled by enemies, or both. Egypt fulfilled these conditions in a high degree."

Here, if we don't demand it too strictly, we can discern the circumscription theory in a nutshell. But there was more. Spencer continued:

"Governmental force was unimpeded by physical obstacles within the occupied area; and escape from it into adjacent desert involved either starvation or robbery and enslavement by wandering hordes."

The Nile valley may have been the most prominent example of these circumscribing conditions but there were other areas that exemplified it as well.

"Then in small areas surrounded by the sea, such as the Sandwich Islands [Hawaii], Tahiti, Tonga, Samoa, where a barrier to flight is formed by a desert of water instead of a desert of sand, the requirements are equally well fulfilled."

Later, in the second volume of *Principles of Sociology* Spencer returned to the same theme.

Whereas, as he had noted earlier, "peoples penned in by barriers are consolidated with facility, I may here add two significant ones not before noted," one being the aforementioned Polynesian islands. "The other is furnished by ancient Peru where, before the time of the Yncas semi-civilized communities had been formed in valleys separated from each other 'on the coast by hot, and almost impassable deserts, and in the interior by lofty mountains or cold or trackless *punas*.'" Here Spencer was drawing on a passage by Ephraim Squier.

But then, by way of contrast with these peoples, who lived in circumscribed environments and could thus be subdued and subordinated with relative ease, Spencer cited the case of the Indians of Popayán and neighboring regions of what is now southern Colombia. Living in a relatively unbounded region they could, according to the 16th-centry Spanish chronicler Cieza de León, retreat "whenever attacked, to other fertile regions" thus avoiding subjugation by a stronger enemy.

What can we conclude about the picture painted here by Herbert Spencer? While it is not the circumscription theory in full regalia, it certainly embodied its essential features.

What was missing from it? There is no explicit mention of unrelenting warfare as the instrument by which certain groups were able to impose their dominance over others and incorporate them into their domain, thus creating larger political units. But of course there can be no doubt that warfare was precisely the instrument Spencer thought as having brought this this development about.

In the passages quoted Spencer does not assert that successive conquests within areas of circumscribed arable land was the way in which *all* the earliest states had emerged. He thus does not present this process, front and center, as a general theory of state formation. Nonetheless given Spencer's proclivity to generalize regularities as broadly as possible it would seem that he was headed in that direction.

The fact that he pointed to the same process as being at work in three widely separated parts of the world but which, nevertheless shared one important characteristic of environmental circumscription suggests that he was well on his way to proposing this as the general mechanism by means of which all pristine states arose.

Now how did all this affect me? In view of the foregoing it became evident that I could no longer think of myself as the sole author of the idea that environmental circumscription lay at the root of all pristine state formation. And I have been careful not to make this claim.

. In a retrospective look at my career in the Swedish anthropological journal *Ethnos*, I declared—with what must have seemed like an ostentatious display of magnanimity—that if I had to share credit for the theory with anyone, there was no one I would rather share it with than Herbert Spencer.

Perhaps this statement requires some amplification. I have long been an admirer of Spencer's writings, having written some half dozen articles about him and edited a selection of the best parts of *The Principles of Sociology*. All this has been done in part to rescue him from the oblivion and opprobrium which, undeservedly, has been his fate.

Now, having thus given Spencer his due, we return to the central question here: To what extent was I familiar with the critical passages in Spencer—the ones quoted above—when, in the mid-1950s I started wrestling with the problem of state formation. I could not begin to deny some familiarity with these passages since I had included them in my selections from *Principles*, which was published in 1967, three years *before* the appearance of "A Theory of the Origin of the State."

More to the point, the question was, had I read them *prior to* the spring of 1957, when the circumscription theory first crystalized in my mind?

I have thought about this question at great length and in doing so have tried to reconstructed when and how Spencer's ideas on state origins could have come into my consciousness, to lodge there, quiescent but not altogether forgotten, ready to spring back to life and be drawn on when I first began dealing with early state formation. Here is the best I could come up with.

Many years ago several blocks of lower 4th Avenue in Manhattan were lined with second-hand book stores. These book stores were a happy hunting ground for anyone looking for out-of-print books on virtually any subject. As a senior in high school, when l was writing a term paper on Captain Cook's first voyage around the world, I made the rounds of these book stores, coming home with an armful of books on the history of the Pacific.

As a political science major in college, I learned of Frank Kent's *The Great Game of Politics,* said to be the best account of the workings of big city machine politics ever written. I had to have that book and I scoured the 4ᵗʰ Avenue bookstores, one after another, until I found it.

Anthropology graduate students at the University of Michigan were handed a ponderous reading list with the items starred which were deemed to be of greatest importance. Such was the dominance of anti-evolutionism in those days that probably no other anthropology departments would have assigned any of Spencer's works, but on our reading list *The Principles of Sociology* received two stars.

Spencer was immensely popular in the late 19ᵗʰ century, especially in the United States. A mountain peak in California and a street in New York City were named after him. But around the turn of the century his writings began to lose favor and as a result large numbers of *The Principles of Sociology* ended up on the shelves of these

4ᵗʰ Avenue book stores. I bought all three volumes of it myself.

This must have been somewhere in the mid-1950s, but I cannot pin down the date any more closely. Just how much of *The Principles* I read at that time I cannot recall. Surely it was much less than the 1,700 pages it contained.

But did my reading include those critical passages, quoted above, discussing restricted environments and their effect on political consolidation? And did Spencer's ideas on state formation strike home at the time, only to remain out of my frontal lobe until, years later, when they may have moved there from my hippocampus, where memories are said to reside?

The pages of *The Principles* I probably read in those early days were most likely those which acquainted me with the importance Spencer assigned to war in building up larger political units. While most other writers stressed the disruptive, *disaggregative* aspects of war, Spencer looked beyond this to war's *aggregative* functions as well.

But of course the political aggregating and consolidating functions of war was only one element of the circumscription theory. Can the assembling of the rest of the pieces of the theory—environmental circumscription and the rest—be traced to my acquaintance with Spencer? I have no recollection that this was the case, but it is certainly not beyond the realm of possibility.

In weighing this possibility it might be useful to consider the following instance. Several years after the publication of "A Theory of the Origin of the State" it suddenly struck me that I had made no mention at all in its pages—as I now wished I had—of an article by Kalervo Oberg that appeared

in the *American Anthropologist* **in 1955**
in which Oberg formally introduced the
concept of the chiefdom into anthropology.
It was a category of great importance,
identifying a stage in political development
that had previously remained overlooked
and unidentified. There was no specific
place for it in the familiar sequence of
Savagery, Barbarism, and Civilization,
which for two centuries had stood as the
three main divisions of social evolution.

I cannot say that Oberg's article was a
definitive link in the chain of ideas that led
me to propose the circumscription theory.
Nevertheless with its emphasis on the
paramount chief as a successful military
leader, which I agree with and considered
significant, it can be said that I thought
Oberg's article to have formed part of the
seedbed of evolutionary ideas out of which

the circumscription theory eventually sprang.

Similarly It is reasonable—perhaps even likely—to suppose that certain passages from Spencer's *The Principles of Sociology* may have formed part of that seedbed. And if in "A Theory of the Origin of the State" I had forgotten to cite Oberg, had I done the same with Spencer?

And yet, recognizing this possibility, it can still be argued that there was no need for my having derived the underlying ideas of the circumscription theory from Spencer. As I described earlier, I had gained a familiarity with the conditions central to the theory from my own experiences in the field and from exposure to the work of others on South American prehistory and ethnology, unaided by anything written by Spencer.

In reflecting on this matter I was reminded

of a similar situation of disputed authorship in which Spencer also figured.

After having formulated the animistic theory of the origin of religion, E. B. Tylor came upon Spencer's "ghost theory," which was similar enough to his own that he accused Spencer of having stolen it from him. In his defense, though, Spencer quoted what Tylor had said a few years earlier in arguing for the plausibility of his animistic theory. "In its main principles," he wrote, "the theory required no great stretch of scientific imagination to arrive at it, inasmuch as it is plainly suggested by the savages themselves in their own accounts of their… religious beliefs. It is not too much to say that, given an unprejudiced student with the means… of making a thorough survey of the evidence, it is three to one that the scheme of the development of religious doctrine and worship he draws up will be an animistic one."

Seizing on these words, Spencer replied, "Mr. Tylor takes the one chance in four, and prefers to think that I did not draw the inferences myself but plagiarized on him."

Well, in regard to the circumscription theory I feel much as Spencer did. If anyone seriously seeking to account for the emergence of the state in South America—or anywhere else—had been in command of the relevant evidence (as I was) the chances would have been three out of four—at the very least—that he would have come up with the same theory.

While on the subject of priorities, let me go further and call attention to the fact that in citing the coast of Peru as providing environmental conditions facilitating political consolidation, Spencer was drawing on observations made earlier by Ephraim Squier, who in turn was basing himself on observations made by the Spanish chronicler Cieza de León three centuries earlier. The line of succession in recognizing the importance of a restricted environment in engendering political integration thus runs from Cieza de León through Ephraim Squier to Herbert Spencer. The circumscription theory can thus claim to have a rather distinguished pedigree!

*   *   *

Before I submitted my article to *Science* I sent a copy of it to John Pfeiffer, a freelance writer well known in the anthropological community. He thought well of it but warned me that because of the theory's reliance on war in advancing political evolution I could expect it to meet with a hostile reception. This hostility was expected to be true especially among archaeologists, many of whom were loath to find evidence of warfare in their excavations, even when it was difficult to overlook. This attitude was amply documented a few years later by Lawrence Keeley, himself an archaeologist, in his book *Warfare Before Civilization*.

As it turned out, though, the expected hostility never materialized. By and large the circumscription theory was received with equanimity by the profession. Not once did I receive an angry letter accusing me of glorifying war or of exaggerating its importance in history. My colleagues seemed to have come to terms with war as a grim reality and to have recognized the essential role it had played in bringing about the great increases in the size and complexity of societies.

One reason for the theory's calm reception, I suggest, is that it faced no entrenched opposition. That is too say that there was no reigning theory of state origins e to feel itself challenged by the newcomer.

And so gradually the circumscription theory made its way until it has become standard fare in anthropology, being cited and discussed in most introductory textbooks. My colleague Craig Morris once told me—and I cannot vouch for the accuracy of his statement—that "A Theory of the Origin of the State" was, for a time, the most frequently cited article in anthropology.

That does not mean, of course, that the theory has met with universal acceptance. In that regard I have been curious to see how it has been regarded by various segments of the profession. I have been particularly interested to see the reaction to it by two groups of anthropologists, neither of which lies in the mainstream of the discipline.

I have in mind the postmodernists and Marxist anthropologists. Its reception by each can be characterized by profound silence.

It is probably no exaggeration to say that most postmodernists are serenely unaware of the theory's existence. After all, their concerns seem to be with more ethereal matters belonging to the parallel universe in where they spend much of their time. Indeed, has anyone even *heard* of a postmodernist theory of how the state began?

Similarly, Marxist anthropologists seem to give the circumscription theory very short shrift, appearing to assign it no significant role in bringing the early state into existence. Could that be because the theory makes no use at all of the dialectic, considered by orthodox Marxists to be the touchstone of proper thinking, especially when it comes to explaining the process of social change?

We also have the puzzling fact that in interpreting the past, Marxists, who purportedly swear allegiance to historical materialism, still turn a blind eye to a theory that places warfare in the forefront of political transformation. Yet what could be more material than the clash of arms?

And this avoidance of warfare as a dynamic element in history occurs despite the fact that Frederick Engels saw clearly the significant role war had played in the development of chiefdoms (as they are now called) among the ancient Germans.

Of this downplaying of war by Marxist anthropologists I will cite just one example—the work of Antonio Gilman, a Marxist archaeologist, whose survey of the province of Albacete in southern Spain led to the locating of more than a hundred fortified sites. Yet Gilman failed to cite war as a major factor in the emergence of chiefdoms in that part of Spain.

There appears to be here an inconsistency of sorts. On the one hand, Marxists are quick to embrace *struggle* as a major factor in social change when it occurs *within* a society—the celebrated class struggle being the familiar example. But still they discount it when it comes to the struggle *between* societies—namely, warfare.

Nevertheless, even without the support and approval of Marxist scholars, the circumscription theory has steadily made headway among theories of state origins. On two occasions an entire issue of a social science journal—*The American Behavioral Scientist* (1988) and *Social Evolution & History* (2012)—has been devoted to the theory.

The circumstances surrounding its

publication in the second of the two journals deserve special mention.

In the years immediately following its original publication, "A Theory of the Origin of the State," I continued to be satisfied with the circumscription theory as it stood. But over time I began to find a few places where the theory could be refined, qualified, or supplemented. Not until after the year 2000 though did I sit down and begin an actual revision of the original article. When I finally finished it I entitled it "The Circumscription Theory: A Clarification, Amplification, and Reformulation." My first thought was to submit it to *Current Anthropology* because I liked the "CA treatment" it accorded the major articles published in each issue, which consisted of farming out the article to a number of specialists in its field and then including their critical comments, along with the author's rebuttal, in the same issue of the journal. This procedure assured a thorough airing of virtually all aspects of the subject treated by the article.

But before submitting my article to *Current Anthropology* I decided to send a copy to Dmitri Bondarenko, one of the three co-editors of *Social Evolution & History,* a Russian journal published entirely in English. I knew Dmitri personally and we shared a deep interest in political evolution, so it seemed to me he might like to read my current views on early state formation. As it turned out, he not only wanted to read my article, he actually offered to publish it in his journal.

I jumped at the offer since I had no assurance *Current Anthropology* would accept my paper, and, as the saying goes, a bird in the hand is worth two in the bush—especially when that "bird" happens to be the best journal of its kind in the world.

But there was a condition attached to Dmitri's offer. My article would be sent out to a number of specialists in the subject for their critical comments, which would be printed on the pages immediately following my article—just as in *Current Anthropology.* I would also have a chance to reply to my critics. Dmitri made it clear, however, that he wanted me to respond to the critics, not *en masse,* as is usually done, but to each one of them individually.

All well and good, I thought, assuming there would be no more than eight or ten sets of comments to deal with, imposing no great burden on me.

However, in the end there were no fewer than 22 sets of comments, and by the time I had finished responding to them all I had amassed some 92 manuscript pages of comments, providing, it would seem, as much text material as was beeded to justify devoting an entire issue to my article.

In the pages of *Social Evolution & History* the elaborated restatement of the circumscription theory received a thorough scrutiny—an acid bath, in fact. It had been carefully read and commented on by an international coterie of scholars, with widely differing experiences and points of view. Their remarks served to file down whatever rough edges remained in the theory. Nuances were pointed out, exceptions were noted, qualifications were spelled out.

Taken account of, the reviewers' comment helped make the circumscription theory tighter and leaner, better able to deal with the seeming anomalies encountered in dealing with a broad spectrum of states and their origins.

For example, I was made to see that under special circumstances—uncommon though they might be—states could emerge as the result of repeated wars undertaken even in the absence of environmental circumscription, resource concentration, or population pressure.

Such exceptions would surely have gladdened the heart of C. W. M. Hart, my old colleague, who was the first person ever to hear me speak of the circumscription theory. But any of what Hart might speak of as anomalies or aberrations of state for formations could not obscure the fact that most primary states had arisen under the conditions specified by the theory. Thus less noble or not, the *rule* and not the exception, had operated in a great preponderance of cases.

And with that, I have nothing further to say about state origins. For more than half a century I have given the subject all I had to give.

That of course does not mean that no further refinements and improvements can be made in our understanding of how the early state emerged. Some advances have already been made along these lines, such as the elegant mathematical elaborations of the circumscription theory proposed by my friend Robert Bates Graber, now professor emeritus of anthropology at Truman State University.

And no doubt other enhancements to the theory are to come at the hands of those who choose to set aside lesser matters and devote themselves to the great problem of how the state arose.

If the circumscription theory has accomplished anything it is to help construct the "exoskeleton" of the early state. To this skeleton though much remains to be added.

The "soft tissue" and "internal organs"... the institutions of state society continue to demand our attention. We leave these in nascent form and look forward to seeing them worked out, thus advancing our grasp of the development of state society.